JUNIOR PET CARE

PUPPIES

ZUZA VRBOVA

Photography Susan C. Miller
Hugh Nicholas
Illustration Robert McAulay
Reading and Child Psychology Consultant
Dr. David Lewis

ACKNOWLEDGMENTS

With special thanks to Jenny Toft at Pet Bowl, Craig Dellow and Lesley Sharpe; Mrs. Lang; Mr. and Mrs. Hedges; Wood Green Animal Shelter.

Library of Congress #89-52052

Distributed in the UNITED STATES by T.F.H. Publications, Inc., One T.F.H. Plaza, Neptune City, NJ 07753; in CANADA to the Pet Trade by H & L Pet Supplies Inc., 27 Kingston Crescent, Kitchener, Ontario N2B 2T6; Rolf C. Hagen Ltd., 3225 Sartelon Street, Montreal 382 Quebec; in CANADA to the Book Trade by Macmillan of Canada (A Division of Canada Publishing Corporation), 164 Commander Boulevard, Agincourt, Ontario M1S 3C7; in ENGLAND by T.F.H. Publications, The Spinney, Parklands, Portsmouth PO7 6AR; in AUSTRALIA AND THE SOUTH PACIFIC by T.F.H. (Australia) Pty. Ltd., Box 149, Brookvale 2100 N.S.W., Australia; in NEW ZEALAND by Ross Haines & Son, Ltd., 82 D Elizabeth Knox Place, Panmure, Auckland, New Zealand; in the PHILIPPINES by Bio-Research, 5 Lippay Street, San Lorenzo Village, Makati Rizal; in SOUTH AFRICA by Multipet Pty. Ltd., Box 235 New Germany, South Africa 3620. Published by T.F.H. Publications, Inc. Manufactured in the United States of America by T.F.H. Publications, Inc.

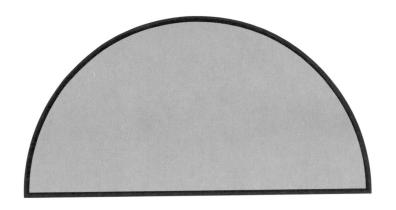

CONTENTS

NOTE TO PARENTS

PUPPIES allows children to find out what sort of animals puppies really are. By encouraging children to watch a puppy's behavior and understand the reasons for it, **PUPPIES** will enable children to care for and train their new pet properly. The book has been specially written for children of age 8 years and older, and will help form a lasting bond between the pup and its owner.

YOU AND YOUR PUPPY

Having a young puppy will take up nearly as much of your family's time as a new baby would. At first, the puppy will need a lot of looking after.

It will grow up and be part of the family for the rest of its life. Many dogs live for about fourteen years and need to be cared for every day of their lives.

You will have to play with your puppy, train it, take it for walks and groom it. In return for the care and affection that you give your puppy, it will quickly become your most loyal friend. It will be ready to protect and look after you, too.

The origins of dogs

Out of all the animals that we keep, only dogs are intelligent enough and friendly enough to be trained to live and work closely with people. To understand your puppy properly you must know what sort of animal it really is. Dogs are descended from wolves and in the wild their behavior was similar to wolves'—hunting and

killing other animals for food.

Outwardly, your puppy will appear very different from a young wolf but in some ways, it actually behaves very much like a wolf. If you are aware of this it will be much easier for you to understand your puppy's ways and habits—the way it might sniff everything and roll over on its back, for example. Understanding your puppy's natural **instincts** will make it easier for you to train it.

KINDS OF PUPPIES

There are many different kinds of puppies to choose from. Some are big and some are small; some have long ears that hang down and some have pricked-up, erect ears. Some have curly tails, some have long, flowing tails; their fur can be long or short and vary in color. Besides the physical differences, all dogs have different personalities.

First of all you must decide whether or not you would like a **pedigreed** puppy. A pedigree is a

You can be sure of having lots of fun with your puppy whatever kind it is.

puppy's family tree. It is a record of the puppy's parents, grandparents and great grandparents that were all of the same particular breed, for example Labrador, German Shepherd, Chihuahua.

All the dogs of one breed look alike and basically behave and respond to people in a similar way. Once you become interested in dogs you will soon learn to recognize lots of different breeds.

If you buy a pedigreed puppy, you will have a good idea of how big it

All puppies are cute, whether they are pure-bred or cross-bred.

Jack Russell Terriers grow up into small and very lively dogs.

will be and what it will be like when it grows up into an adult dog. You will be given its pedigree history, written down on a special certificate.

A puppy with parents of the same breed is **pure-bred.** If a puppy's parents are of different breeds it means that it is **cross-bred.** A **mongrel** is a puppy of mixed breed whose parents are either not known or are cross-bred.

Cocker Spaniels settle into a home well and can be trained easily.

Pedigreed puppies

Each breed of dog has definite qualities in terms of its size and temperament because it was originally bred to help us and fulfill a special purpose.

Hounds are long-legged fast runners because they were used to hunt other animals. For example, Afghan Hounds were used for hunting leopards; greyhounds were used for hunting hare and deer. They can be difficult to train because they are quick to run off after scents.

Terriers generally are small dogs that were used for hunting. They were kept on huge estates and farms to catch animals like foxes that might have been a nuisance. Terriers are energetic, loyal companions and make reliable house dogs. They may be, however, fierce to strangers.

Gundogs are trained to help find and bring back birds that have been shot down. They are obedient, easy to train and dependable dogs like the different types of pointers, setters, retrievers and spaniels.

Working dogs can either be trained to herd sheep or cattle or to guard people and their houses. They are usually big dogs like the Doberman and German Shepherd. Some work-

A Doberman will grow into a big dog that is alert and forceful. It is good for protecting your house and needs firm training, right from the start.

ing dogs, like the husky, are used for pulling sleighs; some, like the St. Bernard and Newfoundland, help to find and rescue people. They are country dogs and need lots of space.

Toy dogs are small dogs that do not need much exercise. Some popular toy breeds are dogs like the Pekingese, Pomeranian and Yorkshire Terrier. They are delicate, excitable dogs; they should definitely not be regarded as toys.

The size of your puppy

Dogs have a very wide range of sizes. Some puppies look small when they are very young but they may grow up into great big dogs. If you buy a puppy of a particular breed, you will know roughly how big it will grow up to be. If you buy a mongrel, you will not be able to tell how big it will be as an adult dog, even if you see the mother.

Generally, the large breeds are good with children and make good

Dachshunds (above) have long bodies and long ears that hang down.

The Australian Shepherd quickly grows into a dog which might be too energetic for young children.

guard dogs too. But, they are very strong and can easily knock a child down—even if they are only trying to be friendly. Also, large dogs need a lot of space in the house and yard and a big open space nearby for walks.

Besides needing plenty of exercise, they need a lot of food.

Some small dogs, although they need less food and space, can be surprisingly fierce.

Choosing a puppy

When you go to a pet store to buy your puppy, you should choose a lively looking one that seems to be friendly, alert, playful and interested

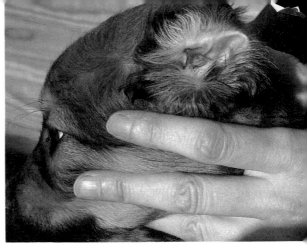

Your new puppy's eyes should be clear and bright. Look closely at its ears—they should be clean and its mouth should be a healthy-looking pink.

in you. Try not to choose a very bold pup as it may turn out to be difficult to train later on. On the other hand, a shy pup might stay shy and timid all of its life.

Besides thinking about the personality of your puppy, you should make sure that the puppy you choose is a healthy one. It should have bright eyes and a clean coat, ears and nose.

19

PREPARING
FOR
A PUPPY

Before you bring your new puppy home, you will need to buy some things for it to make it comfortable and settle it in. It is like having to buy a crib and some clothes for a new baby. But remember, a puppy is not like a baby at all but more like a small, tame wolf.

Bring the puppy home

Your new puppy should be about eight weeks old when you buy it. It will not be old enough to walk home with you. Its only experience of life will have been being with its mother, brothers and sisters.

When you bring the puppy home you should take a special carrying basket or a strong box with you which should be lined with newspaper. Your puppy will feel safe tucked up in a warm, cozy box on the way to its new home.

Special carriers let you travel safely with your puppy.

Your puppy's bed

One of the first things you need to buy a puppy is its own bed. At first, it is probably best to buy a durable plastic bed. This kind is easy to wash and keep clean and the plastic is hard enough not to be damaged by your puppy's attempts to chew it up.

Or you can simply use a cardboard box. The bed should be lined with a soft washable blanket on top of newspaper. It must be big enough for your puppy to curl up in comfortably. Once your puppy is fully grown you might need to buy it a bigger bed.

Think carefully about where you are going to put the bed. Your puppy will be spending plenty of time in it— puppies usually have more than 14 hours of sleep a day—so you should

You can buy food and water bowls that are stable so that your puppy will not tip them.

Gumabone flying disks last longer than plastic flying disks and have a special smell that dogs like, even though we can't detect it.

try to keep the bed away from any drafts and noise.

Privacy for your puppy

Every puppy needs a place of its own. The bed will be your puppy's own place in the house, where it can be away from the rest of the family. Your puppy will probably like to hide its favorite toys or bones there and it will go there when it wants to be by itself. It is like you having your own bedroom to go into when you want to be on your own. You should never leave your puppy alone all day but quiet periods are good for a puppy.

A collar

One of the first things your puppy will need is a collar and leash. The collar should be loose enough for two of your fingers to fit inside when the puppy is wearing it. As your puppy grows it will need a bigger and stronger leash and collar. It is a good idea to buy a tag with your puppy's name and address on it to attach to its collar.

Toys

A big bone is a natural plaything for

a puppy. Also, bones are good for a
puppy to chew on because they help
to keep the puppy's teeth clean and
exercise the jaw. Give your puppy
only big, raw marrow bones. Chicken
bones and other small, sharp bones
are dangerous.

Dog chews from a pet store are
good, safe substitutes for real cooked
bones because they do not have frag-
ments that may splinter and that the
dog may swallow. There are lots of
different kinds of puppy toys and
treats that you can buy in pet stores.

How to Hold Your Puppy

Like babies, dogs prefer to be held firmly and securely. You should support your puppy's body with both hands and hold it close to your body.

Grooming

The amount of grooming needed by a puppy depends on its coat type. But all puppies should be groomed a little every day because it gets them used to being handled and examined. Long–coated puppies that do need thorough grooming all their lives will learn to accept it as part of their daily routine.

Grooming your puppy is important because it removes mud, dead skin and loose hairs and prevents the coat from becoming tangled and matted. Also it massages the skin and at the same time gives you a chance to check that your puppy has no skin diseases or fleas.

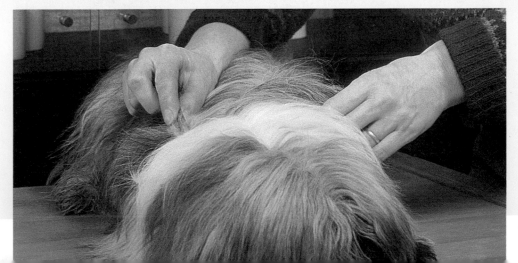

FEEDING
YOUR PUPPY

In the wild, dogs have to search and hunt for food, so they eat as much as possible when they find it. Pet dogs do the same but it is not kind to let your puppy eat too much at once or to leave it for too long without food.

Just like you, puppies need a variety of food to keep them fit and healthy. They need a mixture of meat, cereals and warm milk. **Cereals** are foods like cooked rice, brown bread and puppy meal.

Young puppies, between two and four months old, need four meals a day. At first, you can give your puppy some fresh, chopped-up and cooked meat or fish. Dog biscuits, cereals and warm milk are also very good for young pups. It is best not to give milk and meat in the same meal. This will be too rich for your puppy.

At four to ten months your puppy will only need to have three bigger meals a day. You can make the meals

A good diet will help to keep your puppy healthy and looking his best.

bigger by adding more meat and biscuits but less milk. It is best to feed your puppy at the same times every day and in the same place. Try not to give your puppy any food between meals, or too many treats—especially not sweet ones that are bad for your puppy's teeth. Dogs are greedy and will beg for food when you are eating even if they are not hungry. Do not give your puppy any of your meal as it will encourage this behavior right from the start.

If you watch your puppy eating,

you will see that it does not chew its food very much. Adult dogs have big stomachs which can take large lumps of food. They need to rest after a meal to digest their food.

Although you should not give your puppy food between meals, you must leave a bowl of fresh water out so your puppy can have a drink whenever it needs to. It is especially important for your puppy to have plenty of water if you have fed it any dried food.

By the time a large dog is more than ten months old, it will be happy with one large meal and one much smaller meal every day. Small dogs, though, will still need two meals a day. The amount of food a grown dog needs varies enormously and depends on its size. For example, some dogs can be left with dry food all day, nibbling as they wish, but others would eat the whole thing right away. If your dog is the greedy sort, it is not advisable to leave him food to snack on!

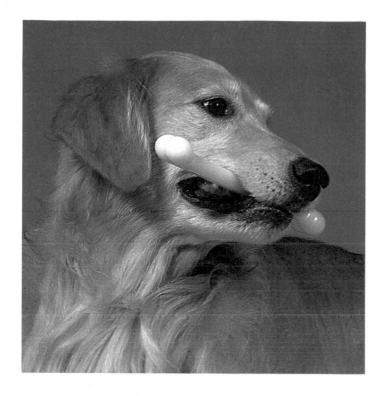

Dogs like to play with and chew on bones. Nylabone products, like the one shown in the picture, are healthier and safer for puppies than real bones. Unlike natural bones, Nylabone chew products do not wear away your puppy's teeth.

Canned food

At first, it is best to feed your puppy the kind of food it has been used to, otherwise it might develop an upset stomach. With some canned or semi-moist foods you need to give your puppy extra cereal, such as dog biscuits. Other brands contain all the kinds of food that your puppy needs in the correct proportions. To be sure that your puppy has the right foods, check the feeding instructions on the label.

CARING
FOR
YOUR PUPPY

When dogs lived in the wild, they lived in groups, called **packs**, and each pack had a leader dog. Your puppy will see you as its leader and will expect to obey you.

A puppy cannot understand what you are saying but it can interpret and remember the sounds and tones of your voice. It can remember the sounds of certain commands, like "No" and the sound of its name, but it cannot understand language.

If your puppy is naughty, never hit it or shout at it. The first time you need to scold your puppy, just say "No" in a stern voice. The puppy will then associate the word "No" with doing something wrong.

Toilet training

Your puppy is most likely to need to relieve itself when it wakes up in the morning, and after each meal or drink. When it wants to go, it will probably sniff the floor and circle around. As soon as you see your puppy doing this, pick it up and put

Keep your puppy away from other dogs until it has been vaccinated.

it outside. If it manages to go to the bathroom, praise it and make a big fuss over it.

If you catch your puppy making a puddle inside, say "No" firmly. It will know by the sound of your voice that it has done the wrong thing. Clean up any mess and always wash your hands afterwards.

Vaccinations

A vaccination is an injection that the vet will give your puppy. It will protect the puppy against the most serious diseases that dogs can suffer from.

As a general rule, all puppies should be vaccinated before they start going out for walks or mixing with other dogs. It is completely safe for the vet to give a puppy a vaccination. Usually there are no side effects after the injection but some puppies might feel a little drowsy afterwards.

The usual procedure is for the puppy to receive two injections. The first one is given when the puppy is about eight weeks old and the second injection is given when the puppy is about 12 weeks old.

Vaccines do not give life-long protection against diseases, so your puppy will need "booster" injections every year. Depending on where you live, vaccination against a disease called **rabies** may be compulsory (required).

Your playful puppy

Puppies love to play with anything. They learn and get exercise by playing. Some puppies like to play hide and seek with a toy that you hide. Many enjoy fetching and returning the catch. If you throw a stick, they will fetch it and bring it back to you. This is fun and good exercise for your puppy. Some like playing tug-of-war with you. But be careful that your puppy does not damage its teeth or hurt its mouth. Also, if you play with sticks, make sure that they are not sharp or have nails sticking out. Never throw stones. Your puppy may swallow them or hurt its teeth.

During the first few months, the only outdoor playground for your

puppy will be your backyard. Try and make sure that it is enclosed and as "puppy-proof" as possible so that your puppy can enjoy some play in the fresh air, but cannot escape onto a nearby road.

Playing with your puppy is good fun for both of you. The toys you play with must be safe, though.

Early leash training
During the first few months of a puppy's life it will need to be kept away from other dogs and even away from places where other dogs might have been. This is a sensible rule because before the vaccination program is complete, your puppy might catch an illness from another dog. For this

reason, even going out for short walks is not a good idea before the puppy is at least 14 weeks old.

But as the puppy grows older, it is a good idea for you to get it used to wearing a collar and being held on a leash. At first, you can try putting a collar on the puppy for short periods.

If your puppy does not like having a collar on, put the collar on before feeding time so that the pleasure of the meal will take your puppy's mind away from wearing the collar.

When your puppy accepts having its collar on without making a fuss, you can introduce the puppy to the leash. Fix it onto the collar for short periods until the puppy becomes used to that, too.

This puppy is getting used to wearing a leash while eating.

Leash Training

Hold the leash lightly, with both hands, with the puppy on your left hand side.

This puppy is being trained to "walk to heel" across the road.

Like you, your puppy will have lots of fun on vacation.

Going on vacation

Taking your dog on vacation means you will have to watch it carefully. It will be in a strange place and although you will probably have a good time running around with lots of open country and space, you must be able to control it properly so that it does not run off and disappear.

A country dog may be frightened by town traffic and a town dog may get very excited in the country and might start chasing farm animals. To help your puppy settle in, take along its bed and feeding bowls.

If your puppy cannot go with you on vacation and if there is no one to look after it, you will have to take it to a boarding kennel. Your puppy will have to be booked in before you go away and you will have to show a vaccination certificate. Most dogs are happy in kennels once their owners are out of sight.

Most puppies settle well into a well-run boarding kennel after a few days.

Clipping and trimming

Puppies such as Poodles and some terriers need clipping and should be taken to a pet beauty parlor.

Bathing is not normally necessary for puppies under six months. If you need to, you can rub your puppy down with a towel. If your puppy does get very dirty you will have to give it a bath. Use a special dog shampoo and rinse it off thoroughly. Dry your puppy with a towel and finish drying with a hairdryer.

Traveling by car

It is a good idea to get your puppy used to being in the car. Most dogs love car rides if they are used to them. Begin by taking your puppy on short trips. Sometimes puppies are carsick on their first few journeys.

If your puppy only goes in the car to the veterinarian's it will connect the car with having an injection or an upsetting day in the waiting room with lots of other animals.

Never leave your puppy alone in a

Tooth Care

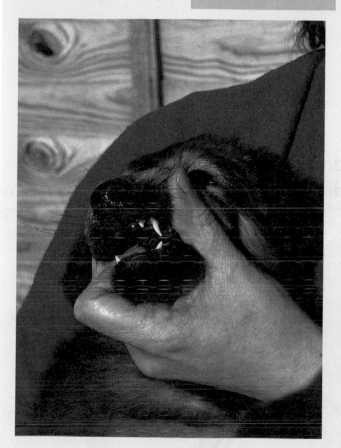

All puppies benefit from having their teeth checked on a regular basis. It is important to encourage your puppy to open its mouth for you from an early age so that it will do so later on.

car with the windows closed, especially on a hot day. Also do not allow your puppy to stick its head out of the window while the car is moving.

YOUR PUPPY'S HEALTH

If your puppy suddenly starts to behave differently or strangely, it may be ill. If you notice that your puppy has lost its appetite and does not eat for more than two days or is being sick regularly, you should take it to the veterinarian.

Worms

If your puppy seems to be much more hungry than usual and yet seems to be becoming thinner, it may have worms. All dogs, especially puppies, need medicine for worms regularly. Your pet store or veterinarian will give you some worm pills.

Scratching

If your puppy scratches a lot, or bites its skin, it is probably trying to get rid of an itch and you should take it to see a veterinarian. He may say that grooming will help. Or, if your puppy has fleas, you will need some flea spray or powder. It is also possible for your puppy to have allergies, in which case the vet will advise you on what to do.

Ear mites

A puppy which scratches or rubs its ears or shakes its head may have ear mites. These are tiny animals that can live in the puppy's ear. You should take it to the vet as soon as possible as a puppy's ears are very delicate.

Diarrhea

This is a very common complaint for puppies. It may be due to the puppy's having eaten some disagreeable food. Sometimes, but very rarely, it might be due to the puppy's having swallowed a stone or marble. If your puppy is sick and has diarrhea for more than two days you should take it to the veterinarian.

GLOSSARY

Cross-bred A puppy is called cross-bred when its parents are each of different breeds.

Instinct A natural inclination or tendency to act or react which is common to all animals of the same species.

Mongrel A puppy of mixed breeds, whose parents are either unknown or cross-breds.

Pack A group of several or many dogs who live, hunt and travel together in the wild.

Pedigree A written record of a pet's ancestry. A pedigreed pet is generally a pure-bred, although cross-breds can also have pedigree papers.

Pure-bred A pure-bred puppy has pure bloodlines, that is, ancestors of the same breed, with no cross-breeding or mongrel heritage in the lines.

Rabies A disease of the nervous system of a dog or puppy; it causes vicious behavior and is very dangerous to both dog and human.